# What is it About the *Horse?*

## *Prose & Poetry*

Author **Shiloh N Blanchard**
Artist **Kristine Blanchard**

Balboa Press books may be ordered through booksellers or by contacting:

Balboa Press
A Division of Hay House
1663 Liberty Drive
Bloomington, IN 47403
www.balboapress.com
844-682-1282

ISBN: 979-8-7652-4798-3 (sc)
ISBN: 979-8-7652-4799-0 (hc)
ISBN: 979-8-7652-4797-6 (e)

Library of Congress Control Number: 2023923370

Print information available on the last page.

Balboa Press rev. date: 01/05/2024

BALBOA.PRESS
A DIVISION OF HAY HOUSE

This book is dedicated to my whole family, both here and now and back when I was young, who have supported my love of horses since I was a child.

# List of Illustrations

Art by Kristine Blanchard
Cover Art, - Butterfly Kiss

# Introduction

We all live in a new age for mankind and a new understanding for all the animals that live here on earth with us. So how does this specifically relate to the horse?

This book was written to help people realize and understand this new age of the horse's mind.

Horses have always been these big, beautiful, and magnificent animals, that helped people with travel and pulling heavy loads. We became used to them as horses who worked for us. We had to keep them healthy and trained for many of the different jobs we needed to have done. In today's world, there is so much more to them once you decide to find it.

Being drawn to spending time with horses is part of a human's desire to be healthier and fulfilled.

I brought to you, in this book, some stories about how to understand and realize what a horse is tenderly capable of. You can call it

enchanting, how horses can communicate back to us, if we can slow down, be quiet and listen.

Horses have become much more than work animals and are worth our love and gratitude.

Enjoy!

# Table of Contents

# Chapter 1

## Gratitude

# *Breath Deep*

The majesty of the horse is legendary,
as it has been throughout time.
But today it is even more so,
when you discover
their incredibly intelligent mind.
Breath deep, take a moment
and say Thank You!
As we connect in love and safety
for the coming ride.

Rising into the saddle with confidence.
Your horse feels safe with you.
Connecting your balance
to the waltz of your horse,
is always such joy to do.

Learning about horses,
and learning to ride,

is also learning with friends.
Friends with both two and four feet,
let's the dimensions of life,
be much more complete.

## *What about Gratitude?*

Do horses understand gratitude,
or even the word?
Do horses know what Thank You means,
whenever the words are heard?
Is it possible that these big, mighty, muscular beasts can think or
understand this highly intelligent concept of Thank You?
What if they can?
Remember, horses are not human. They are sophisticated prey
animals.
So, how can we relate?

We understand gratitude in different ways, from simple words to
enormous hugs, handshakes, kisses and the handwritten phrase.
Horses understand energy in different ways; from high and energetic,
to as soft as a gentle neigh.
What about gratitude? Does gratitude have energy?
When you really mean it, from deep in your body, mind, heart, and
soul.
Gratitude has energy our horses know!

Gratitude is the Best Attitude

## *Ode to the Farmers*

Ode to the farmers who grow the hay,
for our Blessings received every day!
All our Blessings we send to you.
Thank you for all the great work you do!

Rumor has it that
we're grateful!
It's true!

# Happy Farmers & Horses

When you dream of a happy place,
you don't often dream of a farm.
But what if you were a horse?
Would the idea send you into alarm?
Working and helping the farmer with chores.
Quietly waiting for feed we adore.
While all the chickens, ducks and geese are so flappy.
How can this idea be happy?

But what if you were a horse on a farm,
and life for you was grand!
Working the hay fields for your winter feed.
Helping pull the plow, so the crops will succeed!
Having a pasture to stretch, run and roll!
Showers in the rain, feeling good for the soul.
Treats of fresh apples for work well done.
Feeling the gratitude under the moon, stars, and sun!

Pulling a carriage for the Christmas Parade,
while kids throw candy for smiles along the way!
Work pays off with a happy serenade,
of the gratitude, that is always portrayed!

# *Ode to the Trainers*

I had no idea I needed a trainer,
when I arrived at the barn with my new young mare.
My girl was quite thin, and her skin was bare of hair.
She just knew, she needed my care!

A veterinarian, along with a farrier for her hooves,
was the start of our new lives together.
With some healthy hay, supplements, and feed,
we helped her feel much better indeed!

My new mare and I were
becoming good friends together,
as I learned how to understand,
that even though I could easily ride her,
she was a handful for me, to lead and command.

That's when it became a no brainer,
I knew I needed a trainer!

Trainers can see how the horse responds to you,

Then can help and teach the both of you,

while you can see, figure out, and feel,

the help the trainers do, is real!

Thank you

# A Day Well Done

Many days are good days,
Spending time with my horse.

When our day is through,
and the rubbing down has begun,
It's a special time for thanks,
of a day well done.
We accomplished a lot, you and I,
while enjoying ourselves, along our ride.

When the rubbing down is done,
and the feeding time has come,
a final soft pet for the day,
brings a big smile our way.

Back at home, with some time for myself,
open a cold one, sit in the easy chair,
and put my feet up.

Aaaaaagh,
A celebration brew,
for a day will done,
Plus,
all the more, good days to come!

# Famous horses in history

Confidence, balance, and nobility are super-power traits that famous leaders in history have learned from the horse.

## Bucephalus or Bucephalas

A young Alexander the Great was with his father, Philip II of Macedonia, looking at horses to purchase, when a beautiful black stallion was brought over to them to view. Everyone liked this horse, but no one could ride it. It did not take long for Alexander to see, that this horse was young and afraid of his own shadow. So, he asked his father for the horse and said he would pay for him, even if he could not ride him. His father agreed. So Alexander walked over and met the stallion, worked on calming him down and turned him around, so Bucephalus couldn't see his own shadow. Alexander mounted up and rode the beautiful black stallion. His father was amazed and very pleased.

The beautiful stallion, Bucephalus, was said to have a white star on his forehead and a bull's head figure on his shoulder, giving him much character. Bucephalus became Alexander the Great's famous

beloved warhorse! Bucephalus was the horse Alexander rode in many of his winning battles, from Greece, all the way to India.

## Burmese

Queen Elizabeth the 2nd is a very well-known horse lover and has been photographed with many horses in her lifetime, along with her famous big horse loving smile!

The Queen was given a beautiful black mare named Burmese by The Royal Canadian Mounted Police, when they learned that the Queen was looking for a new riding horse for herself. Burmese was then carefully trained for the Queen and the Queen was formally presented Burmese in 1969. Burmese was the horse the Queen rode in 18 "Trooping the Colour" Parades in London.

When Burmese became older, the Queen retired her and moved her to Windsor Castle where she could easily visit her friend. Burmese died in 1990 and is honorably buried at Windsor.

## Marengo

Napoleon Bonaparte the Ist of France, named his famous war mount, Marengo after winning the Battle of Marengo in northern Italy during

the Napoleonic War. This battle was fought against the Austrian's who occupied northern Italy, in 1800. Marengo carried Napoleon safely during the battle. Marengo is the gray Arabian with Napoleon, depicted in many beautiful paintings of the two of them together. Marengo was captured at the Battle of Waterloo in 1815, where Napoleon was defeated by the Duke of Wellington from England

## Nelson and Buckskin

General George Washington rode a couple horses during the American Revolution. The beautiful grey Arabian was named Buckskin and became the horse depicted in many of the great paintings we can still see today! Another of General Washington's war horses was Nelson, who was named after a friend who gave the General his horse during the war. Nelson was a tall, beautiful, chestnut Thoroughbred and a great charger during battle! Nelson was a steady horse who could handle the loud battle sounds, and he carried the General safely during the war.

After the war, General Washington retired both Buckskin and Nelson at Mount Vernon. His home in Virginia.

## Traveller

Confederate General Robert E. Lee's most famous horse during the American Civil War was Traveller. A 16- hand, grey American Saddlebred beauty. Traveller was well known for his endurance, plus his speed and courage during battle!

## Cincinnati

Union General, Ulysses S. Grant's most famous horse during the American Civil War was Cincinnati. Ulysses Grant had a love for horses since childhood and excelled in horsemanship while enrolled at West Point. Cincinnati was a 17-hand tall, beautiful chestnut Thoroughbred given to the General for the war effort.
Cincinnati was a gentle horse until the battle sounds started, when he became a great charger!

## Big Red

Big Red was General George S. Patton's favorite horse and became the riderless horse during the General's funeral. Big Red was one of General Patton's personal horses.

George Patton was born in 1885 and had a love for horses. He attended West Point. He went on to play Polo and did Steeplechase. He was an experienced horseman and rider. He entered the 1912 Olympics in Stockholm, Sweden in the Pentathlon, and placed 6th out of 23 in the equestrian part of the event.

In 1916 Patton fought in the first U.S. motorized battle, it was against Poncho Villa. Patton next went into WWI and was part of the new US Tank Corps. When WWII started, Patton commanded the 2nd Corps, and has been said to inspire the use of Tanks for battle, instead of horses. With all the new motorized vehicles available now, war is not a place for horses.

## Appaloosa's

The North American Nez Perce Native people had spotted horses that were able to move quickly and well over the sometimes-rough lands of North America. These horses were very special to the Nez Perce people, as they carried their mounts safely and were a treasured part of their lives.

## America's Wild Horses

Wild horses of America, or Wild Mustangs, can be adopted by people who are willing to care for them.

There are qualification requirements needed to be allowed to adopt a mustang. You also need the desire, stamina, and skills, to work and enjoy them. Horse training from qualified horsemanship trainers is very important.

For more information:
U.S Department of the Interior
Bureau of Land Management
https://www.blm.gov/programs/wild-horse-and-burro/adoption-and-sales/events

Footnote There is much more history to find on these famous horses and people, online and in Wikipedia.

# Chapter 2

# Holidays

## *Horses and Holidays*

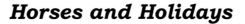

Thankfulness and Giving equal's
Thank You with all my heart!
Heart and Thank You equal's,
How horses help us heal!

Thanksgiving for us people equal's
Thankfulness.
Christmas equal's Giving.
New Year's equal's Happiness,
And
Valentines' equal's
Hearts of Love.

Horses celebrate with us, with
Thankfulness, Giving and Thank Yous,
with their large and beautiful hearts.

Thank You my horses,
For all the Healing you can do!

Merry Christmas

Kristine
Blanchard
©

# A Holiday with Joy

A holiday with joy is a learning time of year.
Time spent with family and friends.

In the past, we'd groom the horses with care,
giving treats of carrots, as the happiness ascends!
Bridles and harnesses all cleaned shiny new,
as we prepare for the big family feast.
Travelling and singing, as the sky shines blue.
The hospitality awaits us, our troubles release!

We've lots to be thankful for and remember what's good.
As in our day to day lives; we always should.
Our ordinary days are working out hardships,
and it's sometimes tough to see eye to eye.

But on this day, a day of Thanksgiving,
we can forget, be happy and eat good pie!

Being together with the happy buffet.
is magic when the theme is living and forgiving,
on this joyous day,
A day of Thanksgiving!

## *The Three Days of Valentines*

Valentines is only one day of the year
and that's just not right.

There should be two or three
to give the time a special might!
Three days of Valentines is exactly
what it should be.

More days of chocolate, hearts, and horses,
cards, dinners, and giggly coffee!

Three days are better than one,
to get us in the right frame of mind.
Three days to be more
thoughtful, thankful, and kind.

# Happy Valentine's Day!

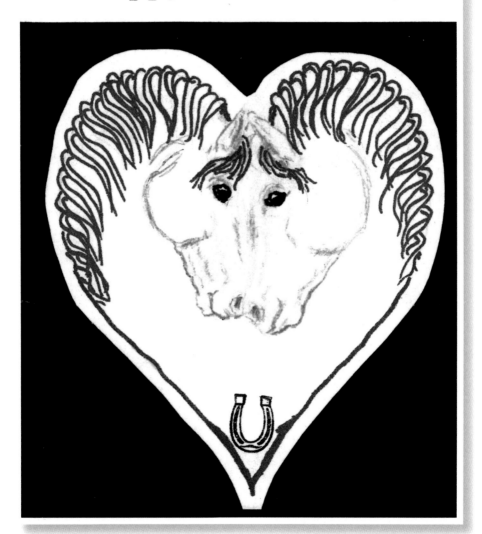

# Chapter 3

## Prayers

## *A Prayer for Us*

A prayer for us is a positive moment,
when we begin our day.
We pray together for understanding
and trust along our way.
Confidence and connection
with a beautiful friend,
brings any little misfortunes
all to an end.

Thank You

# Is it magic or is it love?

Is it magic or is it love?
Understanding the forces from up above.
The power of horse and human's unseen.
Was this connection with us,
already foreseen?

A bond that's so natural and is only felt,
with visions from inside our minds.
Now we're so happy,
we can't help but melt,
with happiness from the Devine.

Is it magic or is it love?
This wonderful feeling from up above.
This gift that came my way,
and filled in times of trauma,
has set me free for happiness every day,
amidst the times of drama.

This gift deserves gratitude, all day long!
Thank you, my friend,
for we'll always belong.
In this magical world of love!

## A Prayer for my Mare

Prayers can happen, my mare taught me that.
Thank you God, for giving us that.
Happily moving, while on a fun ride,
brings us closer together, with every stride.
Nickers, sighs and licking her lips,
lets me know she appreciates my leadership.
Relaxing her guard, while I'm around,
cause she trusts my plans, won't let her down.

My Prayer is that we're always together,
but if we ever part,
whoever owns her next,
can understand the healing,
because she can understand,
your words, thoughts, and feelings,
Especially;
when they come from the heart!

# *All is Well*

All is well.
All is happy for now.
When in doubt,
be strong.
Look your horse in the eyes,
and let love inside!

# Chapter 4

## Nature

## The Walking Beat

Riding the walking beat,
gently swaying side to side.
Relaxing with the gentle breeze,
while mourning doves fly on by.

As the hoofbeats strum the ground,
with their soft and steady beat.
It's Mother Nature's songbook,
playing beautifully.

This book has many sounds,
and can change from day to day.
I'm remembering my favorite days,
with the ever soft, gentle sway.

## *A Ride to Remember*

Riding my horse through the fields of the plains
with the soft summer sun, in the cool green terrain.
Everything came together there.
Our trail ride was only beginning, and
our love was openly felt in the air.

During the ride, a couple geese swam alongside
in the little pond, along the trail.
It's still such delight,
to remember our ride,
it's my very own fairytale!

Along with all this,
wild roses were blooming,
their beautiful scent surrounded the bliss.
I'm blessed with such an enchanting day
to reminisce.

Today, during times of stress,
my worry becomes less and less.
My memory prevails, as I go to this incredible ride.
This time of peace with nature returns,
and comes gliding back into my mind.

## A Treasure of Nature

Gratitude is a journey
A journey of discovery
A journey of seeing
A journey of amazement
A journey of believing

Gratitude is a gift
A gift of learning
A gift of feeling
A gift of amazement
A gift of believing

Gratitude is a wonder
A wonder of understanding
A wonder of blessing
A wonder of amazement
A wonder of believing.

Gratitude is a treasure

A treasure of love

A treasure of believing

A treasure of adventure

A beautiful treasure of nature.

Thank You

~ Anita Blanchard ©

# Chapter 5

## Wonders

# *What is it About the Horse*

What is it about the horse,
that's resting back in our minds.
Why do we instantly know who they are?
The wonderment is one of a kind.
As a child, when we first see a horse
in a drawing, painting, book or tv show,
it's an *Ooooh, Aaaah,* instant remembering,
of times long, long ago!

As we grow and get a chance to be up close and personal,
an overwhelming feeling comes back to life!
We've met before and it seems so natural,
so friendly, beautiful, calming, and masterful.
We flow together in the same light.

There's something about a horse.
It's always been there and always will be.
The scent of their nose and breath is addicting.

Their aura and wisdom is always uplifting.
The horse and human connections live on,
shining together.
Forever as one.

48

# *Horses of Today*

Before motorized vehicles became popular in the early 1900's, we had horses we rode to destinations and horses that pulled carriages and wagons full of people and cargo. Many times, horses were used to carry soldiers into battle. We also used horses to plow the fields and herd beef cattle for our food. Horses had a huge work purpose in our society. For the Native people in America, horses had a huge work purpose with hunting their food, battle, and transportation also.

Nowadays, most of us do not need horses for any work purpose, so why do we still have them?

Horses are still used as transportation for riders, carriages, pulling cargo, plowing fields and herding cattle; but today we know and understand more about the care our horses need to stay healthy and sound.

It is hard to explain; but these days, the thought of owning your own horse, or even taking horseback riding lessons, brings an *"Oooo, Awww, Wow* and *Joy"* to people! It's like we miss them, even if we've

never had the chance to be around them. When you think about it; people and horses have been together for a millennium, or more!

Now-a-days, people like something meaningful to do with their extra time, and many will look at horseback riding or attending a camp to learn more about riding and caring for horses to get the feel for it. For some, they will love it so much, they will continue and become more involved. Horses can easily become the whole deal. In a nutshell, they can teach people commitment, as in the care and feeding of an animal, while enabling exercise from grooming, groundwork, and riding. Riding, if you choose to do so, can become the frosting on the cake!

Many people work with horses and choose not to ride. A way to have fun with horses without riding is with a type of groundwork, called Liberty training.

Liberty is also a fun way to learn how to communicate with a horse. It's how to talk together in the horse's own language. What? Yes! It also lets the horse know that you mean no harm and he or she is safe with you. It's an important step in learning how horses think and it's fun.

Liberty training involves much more than having your horse walk, trot, or canter around you on command. It involves directing your

horse using your own gentle but determined energy. Find a horse trainer who can get you on the path to understanding what to do and enjoy practicing it. Practicing is important.

Learning how to talk, listen and understand your horse with Liberty training, will stay there, when and if you decide to mount up and ride in the saddle, or do some driving work from a cart.

A deep rooted, mind connection is what the horse can give you today. Working together with clear communication skills and trust. Being able to take a moment and think about what you want with your horse, and your horse understands!

We as people, have come a long way with our own abilities with loving and understanding what the horse can bring us.

The Art of Love

Kristine
Blanchard

# My Mare and I

My mare and I are wonderful friends.
She's someone I've always sought.

She understands my every thought,
and lets me know with ease.
When I think negatively, she coughs,
which unlocks the bad, with the force of a loud sneeze!

I know immediately, she's telling me enough.
My thoughts are upsetting and she's calling my bluff.

My beautiful mare with the beautiful mind,
keeps me on the straight and narrow.
Positive thoughts are what's needed,
needed for today and tomorrow.

Thank you, my friend, my beautiful mare,
for knowing and helping me as you do.
It all works out; it all comes true.
My mare,
is my beautiful and answered prayer.

## Can You Read My Mind?

How do you know
the things you do?
Can you read my mind?
How do you intuitively,
already know today,
when I only decided
yesterday?
Really, my beautiful horse;
can you read my mind?

You're an inspiration for me
to do good,
so I can always count on you.
How do you do it, I wonder why,
for I am just a fool.
I'm a fool with people,
when I relate to them,
but with you, I'm learning
to be calm and cool.

My beautiful horse,
you're my Angel
for good thoughts,
as my mind struggles
to be more positive.
To know what it is I want,
works so much more,
than I've ever been taught.

Is there a larger picture
I've yet to discover?
Is there a part of my mind,
I've started to recover?
Or is it all you,
my beautiful horse,
that holds all this wonder,
you've been teaching me,
to quietly uncover.

Thinking of You

## *The pictures inside our minds*

Understanding what our horses know,
explains why events unfold,
that seems to be so far outside the ordinary realms,
that we have always known.

If we can all relax and understand.
Our world is not always as it seems.
Instead, it is able to beautifully expand,
to include how our horses think and dream.

Our horses will feel what we are thinking about,
Big and beautiful or scared with doubt.
Knowing that, our job is now
to remember the safety and enjoyment,
with all the love and patience,
our lives will allow.

# *Communication*

Communication with your horse,
can be interesting indeed.
As there seems to be many
different ways,
to actively achieve.
My horse picked me,
the day we first met,
which sent me driving away,
in a state of dismay!

The magic was magnificent,
and maybe too much,.
for me to understand,
figure out and touch.
What just happened,
and more importantly, why?
Did this broken-down mare,
want me to buy her,
or pass her by?

I spent some time looking
at other horses;
when my cell phone rang.
It was the mare's owner telling me,
more people were coming her way.

I knew it was a sales pitch,
but it gave me an idea,
to bring my young son along,
and watch me take a ride.

Not only did I ride this horse,
remembering her wonderful power,
but my son had his first riding lesson,
from the owner's pretty daughter.

The sale was made!
I looked forward this journey,
with a horse that still needs me to be,
loving, strong, and worthy.

## *Focusing with horses*

Focusing when around animals is an ability, we all should learn to master.

Animals help us learn how to focus, in a unique way that is different than learning how to focus using a machine, such as learning how to drive a car or use a cell phone. With a machine, there is a set of directions. When we buy a new car or phone, it always comes with a manual on how to use it.

Now, take a human baby, and there is no manual that comes with how to teach and care for any individual. We learn and feel it as we go, with trusted advice from people we know. If there is any special care needed - help is there when we take the care, to find it.

Being around horses requires a good ability to focus, and the care to learn.

What is focus?
Is it an art?
Is it a mindset?

Is it attention to detail?

Is it confidence?

Is it concentration?

Is it knowledge?

Is it mastery?

Is it bravery?

Is it love?

Is it all the above?

Horses themselves can be your best manual, as they can become your greatest teacher. They are curious enough to "feel" how you react to them. While we are concentrating on our horse, it creates in us the ability to focus on becoming an alert person who is also calm. Remember the calmness and be willing to be humble enough to always learn.

In other words, the prey animal instinct causes horses to always be aware of any possible danger in the area, and even with you. They can tell if you are having a bad day and that's when focus comes into play. Our days are not always perfect, but when we're around our horses, we can let our problems go and focus on confident calmness. It is art, mastery, love; all of the above!

It is a great confidence builder to focus on having calm energy while still being alert enough to save the day if danger comes your way. When the horse can trust you to be the alert and calm one, they can begin relaxing and calm down also.

Learning this firsthand is always different than reading about it here in this book. Just know to listen and focus on what a good, qualified trainer can tell you about your horse connection, and always ask a question or two if needed.

# *The Mirror*

When I look into the mirror today
What is it I see?
Is it the same as yesterday,
or do I have to wonder?

Is it happy and playful?
is it strong and confident?
Once again,
I have to ponder.

Is the image changing,
as you come up close?
Let me show you some love,
cause that helps the most.

I am the mirror,
and can change as you need.
With you I trust,
your love to take the lead.

# *The Windows*

When you look into their eyes,
you can see this soft glow,
with colors painted in cyan, moss,
burnt sienna, and more.
When you start to ask yourself,
what does it all mean,
what is she trying to convey?
What is he trying to say?

The eyes are windows to the sole,
and all the glory within,
shining out in colors painted vivid,
or colors painted softly,
The artist holds the key,
or does he or she?

Or is it up to you,
to figure out the story behind the beautifully painted eyes,
within a painting of a thousand words,
leaving you with awesome sighs.

## The Eyes Have It

When you look into their eyes,
The wonderment begins to flow.
The feeling of gratitude for being there,
Watching the colors glow.
These burnt sienna browns,
Melt softly into the raw sienna dark.
Keeping this treasure inside ourselves,
Alive till we begin to embark.

A horse's eye is beautiful,
When they look right at you.
Letting you master their look of color,
As we are able to do.
Using oil with our brush,
helps the paint look like new.
We have created the horses' beautiful eye,
in their own beautiful hue.

The windows of the soul show happiness, healing & gratitude!

# Chapter 6

## Fun Times

# *Hoofbeats*

Fun with the beat,
Walking one, two, three, four.

Trotting the two step, is
Faster even more!

Waltzing the canter,
The beat is now sweet.

A full out gallop,
brings the giddy up
hoofbeats
complete!

## Feeling So Good!

Rising into the saddle,
feeling so good.
Can't help but snicker,
when my horse starts to nicker.
Not only nickering,
but also yawning!
As my snickers get louder,
my horse's yawning
becomes larger and longer.
So here we are,
starting our symphony of
nickers, yawns and snickers!

As more friends wonder
what all the snickering is about,
they ride on over and join right in!
Next thing we know,
where did the time go?

Pure enjoyment steals the show,
because now my friend's horses
start yawning and nickering.
And we are all,
laughing and snickering!

Thank You

~ Kristina Blennard

## *Catching up with old friends*

It's so wonderful to see you!
Let's run and play,
like we used to do,
everyday!
We'll help each other with happiness,
as we celebrate our holiday!

When the weather's too hot,
lets run at night.
When the weather is cooler,
we can move with delight.
We can share the good eats,
that give each other might.
While we always know,
we are going to be alright!

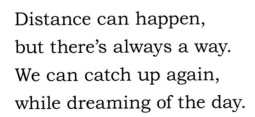

Distance can happen,
but there's always a way.
We can catch up again,
while dreaming of the day.

# *My Sweet Unicorn*

My sweet unicorn, lives in the pastures nearby,
and whenever I get the chance, I try to be by her side.
I ask her how she's been, and she tells me about her day.
Her stories are miraculous, full of saving grace,
Where people have been lost, she helps them find their way.

My sweet unicorn, comes to me in dreams,
helping any concerns I have, leave me like a breeze.
I wake up in peace, ready to start my day,
with thanks for the happiness, she brings along my way.

# The Bushes

The curious mare saw the bushes moving
one calm and sunny morning.
She jumped up and darted away,
In that early part of the day.

But her curiosity got the better of her
as she stepped softly back closer and closer.
When out of the shadows, down close to the ground,
a little brown nose and two twinkling eyes
peered up at her with happy sighs.

Thinking his Mom was finally found,
the little red fox appeared and rolled around!
Carefully, the mare backed away and looked,
at this little one who was playing and sighing.
"What's going on with this happy playing,
so close to me and unafraid?"

The feelings of the two became instantly swayed,
In favor of the friendship that was being made.
For the rest of their lives, they stayed side by side.
In their happy little pasture in the countryside.

# Chapter 7

## Healing Horse Gratitudes

# *How horses help with healing*

Horses have helped all sorts of people, in all sorts of ways!

Many times, just being around horses helps you feel better with their magical, large heart energy.

The musical, swaying movements felt when riding a horse enriches the blood flow in a person's body and can physically help the entire person, whether you have a disability or not!

Horses move with geometric patterns while walking, trotting, cantering, gaiting, and galloping. This greatly helps a person's body and soul in ways that are felt instead of described.

~Equine Therapy

Equine Therapy Farms are around all over the world helping people with many different disabilities.

Some farms have specialty trained people who understand horses and can work well with children with disabilities.

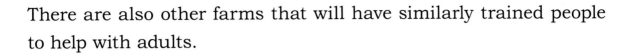

There are also other farms that will have similarly trained people to help with adults.

Many different physical or stressful disorders can benefit from being around horses at an Equine Therapy Farm. Also, many of these farms have websites to help someone find just what they are looking for.

Horses and Ponies continue to be of great help to humans and very much deserve our gratitude.

# Chapter 8

## Something to Think About

## *So Happy*

Woke up this morning at a new place.
What's gonna happen to me now?
People are here and they seem upset.
Upset when they see me so foul.
But hmmm, they're calling me sweety.

Trying to connect to their emotional energy.
Not sure if I should stay or flee.
Wish some muscle was left in my legs,
Then I could decide what's better for me.
Please help me God!

There is a trough nearby filled with water.
Think I'll get to that.

What's that sweet aroma, I recognize the scent!
Could it be, so close and free,
some hay that's meant, just for me!

Right now I'm so happy!
Thank you!
I will stay and appreciate what I have.

For I'm gonna take it, and happily make it,
with this kindness on my behalf.

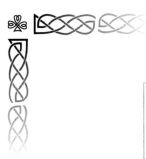

# Appreciation

~ Anita Blanchard ©

# *Something to think about*

Unfortunately, there are abandonment issues in the horse world and for some of the lucky horses, there are good Samaritans that take these horses in.

Many of these Horse Rescue Farms will rehabilitate the horses and put them up for adoption. A good rescue farm will take the time to be sure that the horse and person are a good fit together, before you can purchase, sign the papers, and take the horse home. There is a very good chance a rescued horse could make someone a wonderful partner!

Rescue farms for horses also have Volunteer opportunities for people! Voluntecring is a great way to help yourself and the horses.

If you would like to volunteer at a farm, be sure to tell the farm manager the truth about how well you know and understand horses, then let them decide if you can work directly with the horses or can help in other ways, such as finding donations etc, as many of their

horses need food and veterinary care. The power of giving helps both the horses and people in so many ways!

If you're lucky enough to find a small tack or horse supply store; these places have knowledgeable people who could know the contact info of local horse rescue farms!

Otherwise, ask people at your local horse boarding farm if they know of horse rescue farms nearby.

You can always look for an Equine Horse Rescue Farm online too.

Rescued horses who are now living at their forever homes can become amazing friends and companions, for they can easily understand the power of giving and receiving.

# Chapter 9

## Sympathy

# *Sympathy*

Someone Special who quietly listens,
Someone Special who never lies,
Someone Special who lets you feel wonderful,
Someone Special who shows you in their eyes.

Someone Special who can teach you who you are,
Someone Special who feels the same as you,
Someone Special who shows you how you feel,
Someone Special who can respect and love you too.

Words cannot express, when Someone Special passes,
into the beautiful pastures beyond.
As the horse is always in our heart,
with a strong, unbreakable bond.

## I Already Miss You

I already miss you,
you've been so good to me.
Coming out to brush me,
your love's so easy to see.

You've always been my protector,
even with your disability.
I know you've hatched a plan,
for someone to care for me.

Thank you for your kind words,
I keep hearing in my mind.
I know my own remaining days,
will be with filled,
with your everlasting sunshine.
You're always in my heart,
my loving friend of mine.

# Epilogue

I hope you have enjoyed this book.

It was created to give readers information of "out of the box" ideas on how you and your horse can get along. I've been personally amazed with my own experiences!

It's been an ongoing journey with my mind, connecting to my horse's mind, and so far, the journey has been such a joy for me. So much so, I hope more people will take a little extra quiet time with their horses and appreciate them even more.

Connecting with your horse by thought and eye contact, plus using the power of asking and believing in each of your abilities, can start working before long to happily connect with each other

Remember, only ask for what you want.

~ *Shiloh N. Blanchard*

Shiloh has been drawing and painting horses all her life. Having her own two horses while growing up, gave her a great sense of freedom, while living at the old farm. During her later years she acquired another horse who was a five year old mare.

Because a friend of hers needed some help sorting things out in her life, Shiloh set up some Spirituality inspired afternoons with other friends, and they would meet at one another's houses and read books or talk and ask questions. These small afternoon times together, were extremely helpful for each of us. For me, it awoke, a new sense of being and it has been amazing.

Printed in the United States
by Baker & Taylor Publisher Services